Sick Sentries of Bristle

It gives me grape leisure...

Sick Sentries of Bristle

Derek Robinson

Derek Robinson
With illustrations by Vic Wiltshire

& Vic Wiltshire

COUNTRYSIDE BOOKS
NEWBURY BERKSHIRE

First published 2004
© Derek Robinson and Vic Wiltshire 2004

COUNTRYSIDE BOOKS
3 Catherine Road
Newbury, Berks

To view our complete range of books,
please visit us at
www.countrysidebooks.co.uk

ISBN 1 85306 888 8

Designed by Peter Davies, Nautilus Design

Produced through MRM Associates Ltd., Reading
Printed by J.W. Arrowsmith Ltd., Bristol

Introduction

Little did I think, when a man came through the door with a gun in his hand, that he would be the Muse who would inspire me to create *Sick Sentries of Bristle*!

The man in question was Inspector Grimsby Fish of the Inland Revenue. 'The Treasury needs a fiver to see it through the week,' he said, testing his Kalashnikov with a burst of tracer into a bowl of begonias. 'The Chancellor is at his wits' end.'

'A very short journey for him,' I said. 'And I haven't got a fiver.'

'A couple of quid would help,' he said, reloading.

'I haven't got 50p, and that's my best offer,' I told him. 'And please don't shoot me in the begonias again.'

He turned to my aquarium and cocked the Kalashnikov. 'Either you churn out another Bristle book now, earn some royalties fast, and cough up a fiver in tax,' he said, 'or the big goldfish gets it.'

As he spoke, I felt the rush of inspiration in my veins. 'A romp through the history of Bristle,' I said. 'Six hundred years of the hearty, the smarty and the arty! The haughty, the sporty and the naughty! Not to mention – '

'Exactly,' he said, shooting out the lights. 'Don't mention anything. Write.'

He vanished in a puff of cordite, and the rest is – what else could it be? – history.

Derek Robinson.

Glossary

AFT TRAWL: Taking everything into account.
ANT CHEW?: Haven't you?
ANT SENIOR: Haven't noticed your.

BANK WITS: Big meals.
BARBARA STUFFS: Roughnecks.
BART NIL: Area of Bristle between Reckliff and Lorne's Ill.
BEERS PORT: Do me a favour.
BELL TUP: Less noise.
BIT RAIL: Basic beer.
BLEED NELL!: I'm speechless.
BLIGE: Used to indicate emphasis or emotion; as in 'Blige, Bert, bleed knot, knit?'
BLOOD YELL!: Good grief!
BLOW DEFY KNOW: Haven't got a clue.
BLOW DEFY WILL: Never!
BREN JAM: Basic grub.
BREW NELL: The great Isambard.
BUSTY TUP: Bashed it.

CENSOR YUMA: Laughable.
CHEWS DEE: Follows Monday.
CORE SNOT!: Very stout denial.
CORSETS: Here comes a confident claim.
COUNTS LOUSE: Local authority HQ.
CRATES: Makes or produces.

DEAF KNIT LEA: Certainly; without doubt.
DECK RATED: Given a medal.
DEN: All-purpose Bristle word that gets tacked onto the end of a statement to keep the dust out.
DIESEL LAVA: You'll get a.
DINE FOR: Famished.

FEY SIT: Admit the facts.
FINCHED: Ended.
FORGOTS ACHE!: Dear oh dear.
FURZE: As far as.

GRAPE LEISURE: Much enjoyment.

Glossary

GRAPE WRITTEN: Old steamship.

GUESS A: Fetch a.

GUESS TUCK INTERIM: Give 'im what-for.

HAM RUM: Give 'em hell.

HOLLY DAZE: Vacation.

ICE PECKED: Seems likely.

ICY: It says here.

IDLE: Girl's name with Bristle L.

INCH YEW?: Aren't you?

JELLY DEALS: Gelatinous seafood, fortunately scarce nowadays.

JUICE POSE?: What's your opinion?

LAZE AND GEM: Women and men.

LEVI LOAN: Plea for personal privacy.

MIKE COD: Good Heavens!

MINCE: Short periods of time.

MISSES: The wife.

MOAT WRISTS: Drivers.

MONEY ART NOON: Early in the week.

MONOCLE: Girl's name with Bristle L.

MUNCE: Long periods of time.

MUSTER BIN: The only explanation.

NAB SALUTE: Complete and utter.

NECKS TOP: Destination.

NIGH SCUPPER: Milk and sugar?

NORMAL: Girl's name with Bristle L.

NUMB RATE: Between 7 and 9.

NUTTERS CANDLE: An absolute disgrace.

OFFICE ED: Crazy.

OOZE PAIN?: Where's the money coming from?

PAIN NOAH TENSION: Ignore it.

PAY FORT: Cover the cost.

Glossary

PERRY SHIN: Annoying, maddening, blasted.

POOR TWINE: After-dinner drink.

PORT ZED: Fascinating and mysterious coastal town near Bristle.

POSSE BULL: Can be done.

PUSS UP: Raises, increases.

QUINCE DENSE: Simultaneous happenings.

RACE: Local tax.

RICE CHOIR: I quite agree, mate.

SAM BAGS: Sacks of seaside.

SAM WITCH: Fast food.

SARONG: It's not right.

SAW FLEA: It's very, very, very.

SCAR: Rolled-up tobacco.

SCOLD: Not so hot.

SCONE OUT: Extinguished.

SEAMY CHESS?: Get a load of my torso!

SEIZURE: It's not so difficult.

SERGE ASPER: Notorious baronet.

SHAM BULLS: Cock-up.

SHAWL RIGHT?: How is she?

SICK SENTRIES: 600 years.

SKEWER TEA: Guardian.

SMATTER?: What's your problem?

SNOT: Stout denial.

SNOW: You know.

SNUFF: That'll do.

SOD, KNIT?: Strange, wouldn't you say?

SORRY FINE: Most disturbing.

SOT, KNIT?: Phew, what a scorcher!

STAIN INTENSE: Living under canvas.

STANS TREASON: Commonsense suggests.

STAR CRAVEN MAD: Round the twist.

STEW DUNTS: Undergrads.

SURLY CLOSING: Shut in the afternoon.

TALL DEEP ENDS: Praps. Or praps not.

Glossary

TENOVUS: We're a dozen, less two.
THRONE: Chucked.
TOMB ERICA: Across the Atlantic.
TOUR FREE: Fewer than 4.
TRITE HOMER BOUT: To boast of.
TWANG: To suspend.

WEEDY LIVER: That's us, at the door.
WHY-CELLO: A pale shade of jaundice.

WIDE WYE?: Explain this to me.
WINE CHEW?: Why don't you?
WORSE?: Where is?
WOSS?: What do you?
WOSS SPECK?: What do you expect?
WRECK NON: Depend on.

YULE AFTER: It's your pigeon.

1373

BRISTLE GETS A CHARTER FROM EDWARD III

This turned the city into a county. When asked why, the king said it would keep Sumorsaetesshire apart from Glowcessestersshire; and it might give Wyllettesshire summit to think about, too.

1497

CABOT SAILS FROM BRISTLE FOR AMERICAL

The sturdy west-country name of John Cabot actually concealed the true identity of Giovanni Caboto, an Italian from Genoa, who had to come to Bristle to find a boat. Look it up if you don't believe me.

1574

QUEEN ELIZABETH I VISITS BRISTLE

The queen is said to have given Bristle women the freedom to dry clothes on Brandon Hill, since they were so ugly they'd never get married without this privilege. She was probably jealous. (Who did she marry, anyway?)

1642
COLONEL WASHINGTON'S FIRE-PIKES BREAK THE SIEGE OF BRISTLE

This siege was settling down nicely and looked like having a long run, when Washington cheated by attacking a weak spot in the defences. His men tied blazing straw to their pikes, too. Shocking bad form.

1685

JUDGE JEFFREYS THREATENS TO HANG BRISTLE'S MAYOR FOR KIDNAPPING

The mayor was guilty, but Jeffreys was bottled (as usual), so in the end he just fined him £1,000, which was a lot in those days. 'I'll be glad when this Bloody Assize is over,' the mayor said.

1739

JOHN WESLEY'S OPEN-AIR PREACHING TO KINGSWOOD MINERS SCANDALISES THE BRISTLE GENTRY

Wesley's bosses in the C of E reckoned that open-air services were indecent; but there weren't any churches in Kingswood, and in any case Wesley's congregations ran to thousands.

1780

HOTWELLS SPA – FULL OF THE QUICK AND THE DEAD

Hotwells water did nobody much good, and the visiting invalids keeled over at a rate of knots. The hotelkeepers doubled as undertakers, so they made their money one way or the other.

1804

DIGGING THE NEW CUT TO DIVERT THE AVON PAST THE FLOATING HARBOUR

The estimated cost of the Cut was £200,000, but they hit problems – like solid rock – and it took £580,000 and five years before the 2-mile channel was dug.

1831

Queen Square sacked and Mansion House looted in Bristle riots

The trouble started over Parliamentary reform, but when the mob broke into the Corporation's wine-cellars under the Mansion House, politics took second place. The politicians vanished pretty fast, too.

1843

THE LAUNCHING OF THE S.S. *Great Britain*

A great day for Bristle, or was it? The *Great Britain* was the biggest ship afloat – too big to get back up the Avon, so she had to use Liverpool. Hmm.

1940
BRISTLE IN THE BLITZ

Business went on as usual by day, but it got a bit noisy at night.

2004

SICK SUNDERED YERS ON

Never mind what's happening up there; down here it's usually quicker to walk.

Bristle's Historical Photographs

Shipshape and ... Oh dear

If you think this looks bad, you should have seen the *Demerara*. After the *Great Britain,* she was – at 3,000 tons – the largest steamship that had been built in Bristol. She was meant to leave the Cumberland Basin shortly before high water on 10 November 1851; thus she'd go down the Avon at full tide, much the safest way. But there were delays. Then the steam tug towing her went too fast. The *Demerara* hit a rocky bank on the Avon's right. The tide, ebbing fast, swung her stern until it hit the left bank. Disaster. The Avon was blocked. Mighty efforts got her afloat again. She was sold at a vast loss, and converted to a sailing ship. The *Demerara* wasn't the only big ship to come to grief in the Avon, as this photograph shows, but her fate convinced many shipowners that the Avon – eight miles of twisting, narrow, tidal river – was an evil ending to a voyage, and they looked elsewhere: Gloucester, Liverpool, Cardiff. In any case, Bristol's Floating Harbour – built for ships of 800 tons max – was now far too small. Steam had arrived. By 1848 the Cunard Company had four ships of 2,000 tons. Fine for Liverpool; hopeless for Bristol. And Brunel was building the *Great Eastern*, a 22,000-ton monster. The *Demerara* disaster should have persuaded Bristol City Council that their docks were in the wrong place. For the next 26 years they went on believing that the world would come to them, because it always had. Eventually common sense won, and Avonmouth docks were opened in 1877 – an idea first proposed in 1823. During Victoria's reign, Bristol's leaders had many faults, but galloping haste was not one.

Great Wall of Bristle

Visitors to Bristol looked up and admired the many church spires, St Mary Redcliff above all. If they looked down, they probably saw dirt tracks, because most of the streets were just that, which is why crossing-sweepers did such a steady trade. So building a new road was a big deal. On 20 August 1868, the Mayor and all his pals processed from the Council House to the foot of St Michael's Hill, where he formally opened Perry Road. It linked Park Row with Maudlin Street, and it had cost 50 per cent more than the estimate. So, nothing new there, then. To clear the route, the builders had to tear down a lot of squalid hovels that were ready to fall down anyway. One side of St Michael's Hill – the corner opposite the King David Inn, which still stands, although no longer a pub – got totally demolished. With it went an eight-sided tower, 400 years old, and all that was left of the White Lodge that had been built in a northern corner of the garden of St Bartholomew's Hospital. Nowadays it would be a Grade I listed building and we'd hold a public inquiry. In 1868 it was a ramshackle tower and it got the chop. The handsome wall in the picture reaches almost to the junction of St Michael's Hill and Perry Road, so it seems highly likely that these workers created it in 1868. The wall survives today and looks as sturdy as ever, a tribute to their skill and strength. Observe: not a piece of machinery in sight. Not even a pulley.

Former swamp –
good development potential

Bristol was a bog to start with. The name means 'bridge place' and the easiest place to build a bridge was upstream of the gorge where the land was flat and boggy. So the space at the meeting of the Frome and the Avon got called Town Marsh (as distinct from Canon's Marsh, on the opposite side). It dried out and became a favourite promenade, with a bullring, a bowling green and a tavern. Then, in the spring of 1700, 'masons and bricklayers had invaded the quiet meadow' and begun building 'a handsome square of mansions'. Two years later Queen Anne was in Bath, taking the waters (she had gout), and she agreed to visit Bristol. Thirteen coaches, each pulled by six horses, came via Kingswood. (The Keynsham route was described as 'founderous', meaning it was so muddy you sank up to your knees.) She knighted the mayor, dined while a 100-gun salute boomed from Town Marsh, and was on her way back to Bath by 5 pm. Bristol was happy, and 'to perpetuate the memory' Town Marsh was called Queen Square. Soon 240 trees were planted. In 1823 a proposal to build a Council House in the middle was rejected; just as well, because eight years later half the square went up in flames, in the Bristol Riots. In 1865 the Council wanted to build law courts there; defeated, by 37 votes to 13. But in 1937 the vandals had their way: they cut a main road slap across Queen Square. It didn't last. And the animals? Sheep had grazed here since Tudor times; cattle too. Kept them fat, and the grass short.

High tension

Not true. Isambard Kingdom Brunel was not on holiday when Clifton Suspension Bridge was completed; he was at rest, dead of kidney disease at the age of 53. It was pure chance that brought him to Bristol in the first place. By 1828, his father's attempt to make a tunnel under the Thames at Rotherhithe had ended in failure. When the roof collapsed, Isambard was nearly drowned. He convalesced in Brighton, drinking too much and too often, so his parents sent him to Clifton instead. Nice timing: the Society of Merchant Venturers announced a competition for a bridge over the gorge. By now, Brunel was almost resigned to a life of failure, but the competition revived him. He submitted four designs. Their spans varied from 870 ft to 916 ft. Nowhere in the world had anyone built a suspension bridge so big. Brunel had a struggle to win over the Bridge Committee – he was only 23 – but in the end he succeeded. (Personally, I think they chose the wrong design: Brunel's plan to have the bridge emerge from tunnels on each side of the gorge, with the suspension chains anchored to the rocks above, was marvellously dramatic.) Work began. Brunel actually crossed the gorge in a basket slung under an iron bar. Then came the Bristol Riots of 1831 (Brunel served as a Special Constable). With so much of the city in ruins, the Clifton Bridge scheme was forgotten. Brunel moved on. In 1860, a year after his death, work began again, and the bridge was opened in 1864: a great memorial to a great man, but one he never saw.

Lashings of Nash

This is the scene that launched a thousand Christmas cards, a hundred chocolate boxes, and even a few decorated teapots: Blaise Hamlet, a group of cottages near Blaise Castle House. The house was built by the Harfords, Quaker bankers who liked to prettify their estate with romantic nonsense, such as a thatched dairy, a lovers' leap, and a woodland lodge in the distance because they fancied seeing smoke rise from its chimney. In 1811, Harford asked John Nash to create some estate cottages for his old retainers. Nash was flying high: he was redesigning Regent's Park for the Prince of Wales, and later his credits included Buckingham Palace, the Marble Arch, and Brighton Pavilion. For the Harfords he designed the most romantic and picturesque collection of cottages in England – nine of them around a fairytale green, with a pump in the middle. Each has a hefty chimney (some round, some polygonal) and the roof may be pantile or stone slate or thatch. No two cottages are alike. Blaise Hamlet makes Castle Combe look like Milton Keynes. But Nash knew his stuff. Each cottage was quaint on the outside and comfortable on the inside, with its own loo, an oven, and a copper for laundry. People have lived here happily for nearly 200 years. How many tower blocks of flats will still be standing, let alone admired, 200 years from now?

Hold very tight, please. Ting-ting!

The Lady Mayoress laid the first rail for a Bristol tramway in 1863. Then everything went to hell. The tramway company ran into money trouble, partly because its secretary, John Bingham, was a crook who got 12 months with hard labour. Fast-forward to 1871. The Council decided to build the lines itself, starting with one from St Augustine's Place (the Centre) to Redland. Suddenly the price of iron doubled, and with it the cost of rails. The Council nearly threw in the towel. Then, in 1873, it tried again, doing what Councils everywhere are good at – digging up the road, especially Whiteladies Road. The builders ran out of iron. Whiteladies was left half-blocked for six months, 'to the great wrath of those using the carriage way'. Iron was found, and the tramway was finished in the spring of 1874. Sighs of relief all round. Not for long. Now the tramways committee couldn't get a fair bid from anyone to run the line. Eventually some worthy citizens offered to do it, provided they got some trifling concessions. Such as? Well, they wanted the use of the tramway free for seven years, for a start. 'Preposterous!' the Council cried. Stalemate. But they worked out a compromise: a 21-year lease, the first five free of charge, thereafter a rent rising from £300 to £600 a year. Soon new lines were spreading across the city and, since the Council was paying for their maintenance, it was a damn good deal for the company. There were problems, of course: tradesmen in the suburbs hated trams because they removed customers; the Sabbath-observance people opposed Sunday travel; and the middle classes resented anything that took the working classes past their front door. But the tramways – moving at a steady two horsepower – triumphed.

The word on the street

Victorian newsboys took a pride in their appearance: suits, overcoats, wing collars, ties, even a cravat (extreme right). What look like riding boots were probably leather gaiters, very suitable when half of Bristol's streets were mud. Why this team is selling the *Horfield & Bishopston Record* in Colston Avenue is anybody's guess. 'Free Press' didn't mean the paper was given away. The story goes back to 1711. Newspapers were starting to be popular. Governments hated them. The common people had no right to information. What Parliament did was Parliament's business, and it was Crown copyright. Many an editor went to jail for printing such news. The *Bristol Journal* had the nerve to print the King's Speech at the dissolution of Parliament, and was made to apologise for three weeks, and promise never to offend again.

Then someone in the Treasury had a cunning idea. Tax newspapers! Even one-page news-sheets! Each copy sold had to bear a red stamp costing a halfpenny. This went up steadily. By 1815 the tax was fourpence and *The Times* cost sevenpence. A labourer worked 3 or 4 hours to earn sevenpence. And that wasn't all: every advertisement, no matter how small, was taxed at 3 shillings and sixpence, a week's wage for many. It was even a crime to buy a newspaper and lend it out for hire. The 'tax on knowledge' was abolished in 1855. Now began the era of the Free Press, when newspapers cost a halfpenny or a penny, and they told readers what governments would rather they didn't know. Forget Magna Carta. Democracy began in Britain with a Free Press.

Where there's smoke, there's dung

The idea of a city fire brigade in Bristol is relatively new. On a few old houses, you can still see a plaque depicting the sun, which indicated that it was insured by the Sun Insurance Company. If the place caught fire, the company called out its own part-time firemen. Their job was to protect the property, not to save life. The police kept some escape ladders to rescue people trapped in upper storeys, but they were heavy and cumbersome and not easily moved. Bristol was a busy seaport crowded with warehouses, and it had its share of fires, in particular a big blaze on 24 May 1876 in Christmas Street, near the centre. The insurance companies sent their brigades, but the pumps were manual, and the best pump needed 36 men to work its levers. This was hard labour and it demanded frequent replacements. Christmas Street burned like a beacon. Time for a change. In 1877, Bristol set up its municipal fire brigade and bought a Merryweather Steamer – a steam-driven fire engine which could throw a jet of water 150 feet high and needed only two men to operate. The engine worked by steam but it was pulled by two horses, hired from the Bristol Tramways Company. The city was proud of its Steamer, and the brigade often demonstrated the engine to the public, which is probably what's happening in this very gung-ho performance, taking place, apparently, in the middle of nowhere.

Praise be!

Here's an extraordinary picture of the amazing achievement of one truly great man. On the skyline you can see the outlines of the five homes for orphaned boys and girls, built by George Muller on Ashley Down between 1849 and 1870. Muller was born in Germany in 1805 and (he said) had a riotous youth: 'there was scarcely a sin which I did not commit'. He saw the light, came to England as a student with a London missionary society, went to preach in Devon, then in Bristol. The sight of so many ragged, hungry children running wild in the streets led him to start his life's work. His five homes had room for 2,050 orphans. When you trace the long line of children in this picture, downhill, under the railway line, and beyond, you get a slight idea of the vast challenge he took on – always without money in the bank to do it and always without appealing for donations. The Lord will provide, he believed, and somehow the money arrived when needed. (At his death, the total was just under a million pounds; well over £100 million in today's money.) What's impressive about Muller's orphans is how healthy, well-dressed and well-fed they are. This line is on its way to the annual picnic on Purdown. Each girl has a shawl to sit on and a small cotton bag of sweets and biscuits. Muller died in 1898, aged 92. His homes are no longer orphanages, but Muller's Foundation carries on the good work.

'Damn you!' he explained

Chucking a brick through a window was what passed for serious political comment among male students at Bristol University in the Edwardian period, and this was the window they chucked it through. The year was 1911. The window was in the Queen's Road headquarters of the local suffragette movement. George Wills, son of tobacco tycoon H.O. Wills, gave the University some playing fields at Coombe Dingle. While he was at it, he built a sports pavilion. The suffragettes burned it down. Male students didn't need telling that cricket was more important than the right to vote, and they marched down University Road and attacked the suffragette office. They smashed the windows, trashed the interior, threw out pamphlets, threw in stink bombs, lit a large bonfire and danced around it. The police couldn't tolerate this vandalism – the crowd was holding up traffic – so they sent for the fire brigade, which put out the flames. Everyone went home. It was little wonder that some suffragettes used extreme measures. They had been fighting for the vote since the 1860s. By 1911, the National Union of Women's Suffrage Societies had 200 branches, including Bristol. The police broke up their demonstrations, and not gently. Some 500 members went to jail. (There was even, amazingly, a Women's National Anti-Suffrage League.) In the end, the First World War made the difference: the remarkable work done by women convinced the country, and in 1918 Parliament began extending the vote to women.

Edwardian rush hour

Having soldiers billeted in your house was like renting rooms to male students, except the soldiers always got into fights and never went home in the holidays. But up to Queen Victoria's time, that was the army's usual solution to the problem of finding somewhere for soldiers to live. For obvious reasons, the easiest place to put them was the local inn. The publican resented it, and his customers weren't very happy either. Billeting soldiers in Bristol became such bad news that in 1843 the government bought part of Horfield Court Farm. Four years later it had spent £57,000 – a huge sum in those days – on a barracks big enough for two troops of cavalry and four companies of infantry. It became the home of part of the Gloucestershire Regiment, called simply 'The Garrison'. In the 1840s, Horfield Court Farm was well outside the city boundaries. No doubt the army thought it was a good idea to site the barracks out in the sticks, where the troops had nobody to fight but themselves. Even in this photograph, taken near the barracks in 1910, not much went on at Horfield Common. The horse and cart cheerfully occupy the middle of the road; the pair on the motorcycle combination are enjoying their adventure into Gloucestershire; the sidecar is a basket. Note that half the road is paved with flat cobbles. Progress!

Join now to avoid disappointment

The First World War was still new and exciting when this picture was taken, which may explain some jolly expressions. Many Bristolians cheered the declaration of war in August 1914. They marched up and down, sang patriotic songs, and couldn't wait to get into uniform and biff the Hun. The regulars and the Territorials were soon off to France: the Gloucesters, the North Somerset Yeomanry, the Royal Gloucestershire Hussars, the South Midland Royal Engineers. The rush of civilians swamped the Recruiting Office and the War Office took over the Colston Hall. Many recruits joined 'Bristol's Own' 12th Battalion, the Gloucestershire Regiment. But as autumn faded, so did the volunteering. The Recruiting Office moved out of the Colston Hall. In his excellent *The Forgotten War*, James Belsey quotes from a magazine, *Bristol And The War*. It was so worried about poor recruiting that it wrote:

'Sufficient is not made of the jolly adventuring of soldiering. One would think, to hear some people, that it consisted of nothing but impaling Germans on bayonets and spending the intervals starving and shivering in flooded trenches. Give our modern buccaneers some glimpse of the glories of travel, change of scene, and camp-life … Let the men have a glimpse of the wonderful machinery of war…'

On 3rd September 1916, 'Bristol's Own' battalion joined the Battle of the Somme. In this action, of 913 men, 324 were killed or wounded. Not such a jolly adventure.

Ham? Jam? Thank you, ma'am

I don't know why milkmen, and not other deliverymen, got a reputation for being ultra-friendly to housewives. Is there any evidence? This Co-op milkman looks very respectable, almost managerial. That milk churn, hung between the wheels, must have been heavy when full, and quite a challenge on hills. Maybe the two loops on the front of the cart were for helping hands in an emergency. The photograph is said to have been taken in St John's Lane, Bedminster, probably around the time of the First World War; but it was a typical scene all over Bristol. It's only recently that we fired up our 4 x 4 off-road all-terrain vehicles and drove several miles to supermarkets so that we could herniate ourselves as we loaded up enough grub for a week. Long after the Second World War, delivery vans criss-crossed Bristol every day, delivering milk, bread, fruit and veg. Butchers and grocers routinely delivered to the home: you gave them a note of what you needed, and they did the rest. There were other callers: the rag-and-bone man with his horse and cart; Johnny Onions with strings of onions hanging from his bike; the knife-grinder with his pedal-driven grindstone that would also sharpen garden shears. And a Bristol favourite was Pickup, a fizzy drink that came in a half-gallon, screw-top, pottery pitcher. The Pickup man wouldn't deliver a full one unless you gave him an empty. Printed on it was the stern warning: *This bottle is not sold. Any person detaining or using same will be prosecuted.* I not only detained ours; I'm using it as a doorstop. It's a fair cop, guv, I'll come quietly.

Big deal

Few Mayors of Bristol can have taken the chair in the Council Chamber and surveyed those present over the top of a machine gun, although many may have wished they could. The honour fell to the Mayor on 20 June 1916. A unit of Bristol troops had captured a German machine gun, and they presented it to the city. When hizzonner tired of the weapon it was put on display in the Art Gallery. For all I know it's there still, down in the basement, slightly oiled and waiting to be submitted for the Turner Prize. Military trophies were popular in the First World War. A couple of months after the Armistice, the Royal Navy towed two captured U-boats up the Avon and moored them in the city centre. (In those days the docks extended further than they do now.) They attracted a lot of visitors. Soon after, a small and scruffy tramp steamer, the *Hyderabad*, arrived and brought more crowds out. The newspapers called her a 'mystery ship'; the Admiralty term was 'Q ship'. She looked harmless until a U-boat approached her, when shutters dropped to reveal guns and torpedo tubes, and battle was joined. Zeppelins never reached the West, which probably explains the fascination with a charity auction of bits of a Zeppelin that was wrecked in a bombing raid. One piece of wire, only two inches long, got sold and resold until it made over £30. And the tank? It's British, probably a Mark IV model, on display at Durdham Downs. Don't be fooled by what look like radio aerials. Those are the trailing masts from electric trams. You can just see one tram to the left of 259.

Down the 'Mouth

I showed this picture to a retired docker, Bert Gray, better known as 'Dolly' (all dockers had nicknames), and he reckons it was taken at Avonmouth, probably about the turn of the century because there's no sign of machinery, no conveyor belts taking the bananas ashore. Bert gave me a wealth of detail about dockers' work on Elder & Fyffe's banana boats from the West Indies. You had to be strong. The docker on the gangplank is carrying a 'stem' of bananas, which weighed 100 pounds or more. Before he reached the gangplank he'd carried it out of the hold, which was long and deep. There were two compartments in the hold, upper and lower. Rubbish, such as rotten fruit and dropped stems, fell into the lower, so experienced dockers always tried to work the upper. The gangplanks, or 'shivers', had no guard rails. Surprisingly few dockers stumbled and fell, and those that did usually got fished out. Spiders were big but normally harmless (they ate bananas). Snakes were sometimes found, but every ship kept a mongoose on board to kill the snakes. Unloading bananas was popular work, compared with other cargoes. Dockers got a shilling a day splinter money for unloading timber, sixpence a day sticky money for sugar, and fourpence a day for red or yellow ochre. Rice was one of the least popular, since it usually arrived covered in weevils. But whatever the ship carried, dockers welcomed the work. They were all casual labour and, when 500 or 600 turned up, perhaps only half might be taken on for the day. Bert Gray and his mates earned every penny they made, and then some.

The stuff to give the troops

Bristol had a constantly shifting population of servicemen in the First World War. Some were in training, some in hospital. Some were on leave, some waiting to be shipped overseas. Where did they go in their spare time? The pub, maybe, although opening hours were strictly limited. No Naafi in those days. Many servicemen just hung about, on the streets. It took more than two years for someone to realise they needed a safe place to relax in, out of the rain. That someone was the YMCA. It opened the Dug-Out in Colston Street in May 1917 (the sandbags were decorative, to make the chaps feel at home), and immediately it was such a huge success that the YMCA expanded it to five times the size. There was a large canteen, recreation room, reading room, baths, cloakroom, and beds for up to 230 servicemen. The Dug-Out was open day and night, and in the next two years over a million men passed through its doors. Four hundred volunteers ran the place. They served over 700,000 meals; provided beds for 78,000 men; and organised teas, concerts, visits, and cricket and baseball matches. (By 1918, American troops were in Bristol.) The slouch hats and the bandages in the photograph suggest that some of these men were wounded Australians and/or New Zealanders. The Dug-Out wasn't alone: the YMCA also ran canteens at Avonmouth, Portbury, Hallen, Henbury, Chittening, Horfield, Filton, Albion Shipyard, Bedminster and Kingswood, as well as eight centres for munition workers – a total of at least twenty YMCAs for servicemen and war workers in Bristol. Magnificent.

The Gang Show

Forget the funny hats. The Scout movement was the right idea at the right time. It gave millions of boys exactly what they wanted – the chance to get out of the house, out of the town, and go camping. It taught them how to light a fire with two matches and no paper, how to mix flour and water and cook it into something edible: in short, how to be self-reliant and enjoy an adventure in the country. Two surprising facts. First, that Baden-Powell (hero of the siege of Mafeking) founded the movement, in 1908, only **after** he learned that his military textbook, *Aids to Scouting*, was being used to train boys in woodcraft. Second, that B-P, a career army officer, didn't order anyone to set up a troop of Boy Scouts. He simply founded the movement, and left it to boys themselves to start their own troops – after which he offered plenty of support. The movement spread rapidly throughout Britain and, later, the world. (My local troop was the 126th Bristol, which gives you an idea.) At a guess, this photograph was taken in the early 1920s – those waterbottles look like war surplus to me. Sharp-eyed ex-Scouts will notice the Scoutmaster's puttees, and also the casual tying of the neckerchiefs; obviously the woggle had not yet reached Yate. Some hat-brims are admirably flat; others flop like cabbage-leaves. The trick was a hot iron and a damp cloth, but even a crisp brim didn't last long in the rain, and of course it always rained when the Scouts went to camp. Always.

A boom with a view

That's ten tons of bell. On the hour it booms a lordly E flat over Bristol University. It tells lecturers it's time to clear their throats and start pontificating. It tells professors to put down the crossword and start professing. Above all, it tells students that the pubs are open. Great George is the fourth biggest bell in Britain, and it has the deepest note – deeper even than Big Ben. Before the bell, of course, came the tower it hangs in, and before the tower there was, not a University of Bristol, but a mere University College. 1909 was when Edward VII signed the Royal Charter that got Bristol up and running as a University. It was built (like so much of the city) on fag-ends. Wills Tobacco was a money-making machine, selling a product that the customer obligingly burnt so that he had to buy some more. H.O. Wills had two sons, George and Henry, who wanted to do something big to commemorate the large cheques their father had given to the infant University. The Wills Memorial Building has a tower 215 feet high. King George V opened it in 1925, so Great George probably got hoisted in 1924. The entire building cost a shade more than half a million pounds at 1925 prices. And Wills Tobacco is now a fading memory. Makes you fink, dunnit?

Trial by night

The Blitz was no joke (although plenty of jokes came out of it. Man and wife went to bed during a raid. She kept on and on about the banging of guns and the bursting of shells, until he snapped: 'For goodness sake shut up. How can I get to sleep when you're making such a row?') The big Blitzes were six: 24th/25th November 1940; 2nd/3rd December 1940; 6th/7th December 1940; 3rd/4th January 1941; 16th/17th March 1941; and the last and worst, on the night of Good Friday, 1941. There were many smaller raids. All told, they killed 1,159 people and wounded twice that number; destroyed 2,500 homes and partly damaged 46,000; and blew up or burned down hundreds of historic buildings, such as the Dutch House shown in the photograph. For me, a headstone in Greenbank Cemetery sums up the tragedy of the Bristol Blitz. It tells of the end of a family of seven: William and Carrie Isaacs, both 40; and Joyce, 15; Vera, 13; Willie, 12; Barbara, 10; and Norman, 8. One bomb killed them all. It's easy to guess what made Bristol and Avonmouth a target. The docks and the railway network were crucial to Britain's imports at a time when Germany was hoping to starve us into surrender. So bombing the city centre can be put down to a near-miss of Temple Meads. But what of the repeated bombing of Redland, Clifton, Brislington, Whitehall, Hanham, Southmead, Knowle and a dozen other districts? Even rural spots like Leigh Woods and Long Ashton? What did the Luftwaffe hope to achieve by bombing allotments in St George? The fact is that Bristol was easy to find – just follow the Severn and the Avon – but bomb-aiming in 1940–41 was a primitive business. All too often the Luftwaffe aimed at the biggest fire, which might be a hayrick near Pilning. What seemed to be random bombing was in fact just bungling. But it could hurt just the same.

Severn Beach makes a splash

In the 1930s, Londoners used to take day excursions to Severn Beach. A return ticket from Paddington cost seven shillings and sixpence. Look it up, if you don't believe me. Holidaymakers also came from Manchester, Birmingham, elsewhere. Severn Beach was a throbbing, thrilling oasis of fun and frolic in the dull flatlands of South Gloucestershire. It had a Chinese pagoda, two boat lakes (one with little petrol-engined speedboats), miniature golf, a miniature railway, endless tearooms and icecream stalls, a camp site (where I spent a wet week in a bell tent) and, above all, the Blue Lagoon. This was painted a shimmering Mediterranean blue, and it had a water-slide and a six-level diving stage. It was very big and very popular. The Blue Lagoon was the jewel in the crown of Severn Beach. The resort had a strip of actual beach (still does) but it was very pebbly and all it offered was a view of Wales. What Bristolians (and Londoners) relished was splashing about in the glorious Blue Lagoon. Severn Beach flourished in the 1930s, and it was still doing very nicely in the late forties. But, in the end, nature got the best of it. The Blue Lagoon took its water from the Severn, and filtering out all the mud proved impossible. They just didn't have the technology. Here you see the Blue Lagoon in its heyday. If you're interested, I'm the goodlooking lad about to do a reverse double backward nosedive.

Yer! Payer tension! This

STIFF CUT

is awarded to

. . . .

because he/she is

100% BRISTLE

and you'd better believe me
or diesel get my fist up thy frote.

Grace Tepp-Ford
Bristle's First Lady